Learn to Draw Animals : Pencil Drawings Step by Step

Pencil Drawing Ideas for Absolute
Beginners
How to Draw : Drawing Lessons for
Beginners

by GP EDU

Published by:

GP EDU

© Copyright 2015 – GP EDU

ISBN-13: 978-1507608067
ISBN-10: 1507608063

Table of Contents

How To Draw Eagle

STEP : 1

STEP : 2

STEP : 3

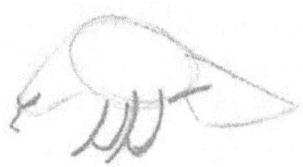

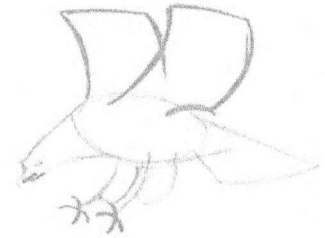

STEP:4

STEP:5

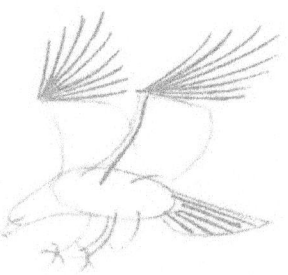

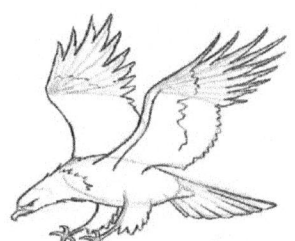

STEP: 6

How To Draw Black Kite

STEP : 1

STEP : 2

STEP: 3

STEP: 4

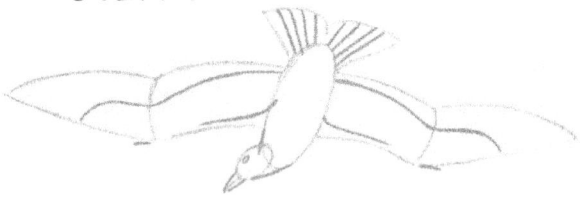

STEP: 5

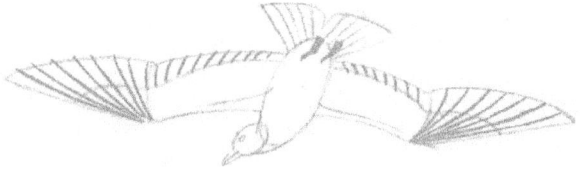

STEP : 6

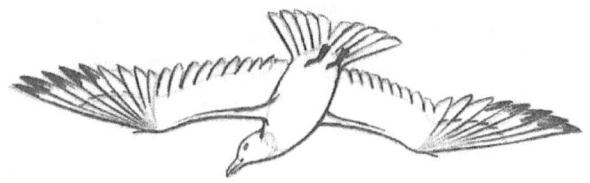

How To Draw A Parrot

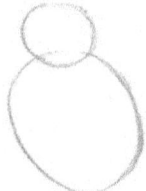

STEP: 1

STEP: 2

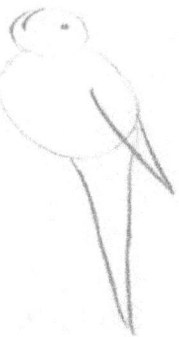

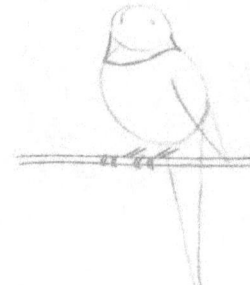

STEP: 3

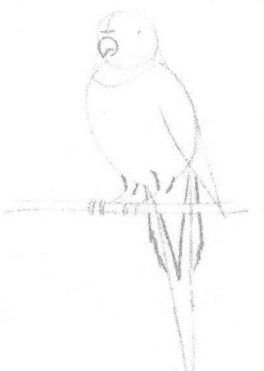

STEP:4

STEP:5

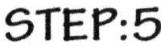

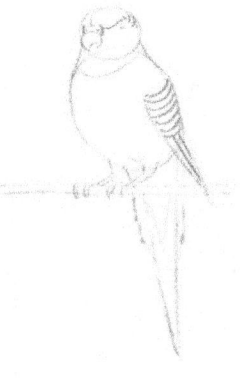

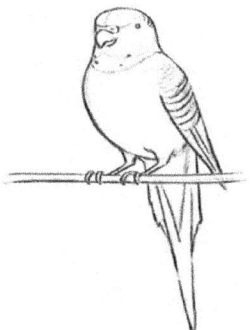

STEP:6

How To Draw Sparrow

STEP:1

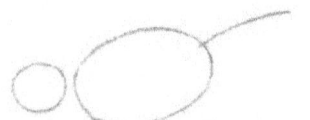

STEP:2

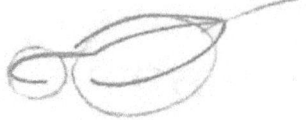

STEP:3

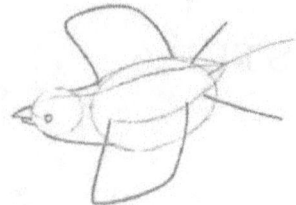

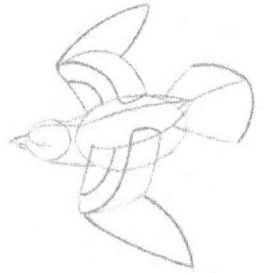

STEP:4

STEP:5

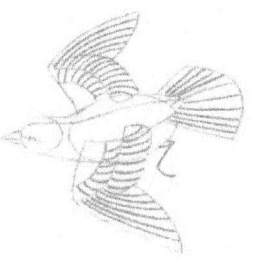

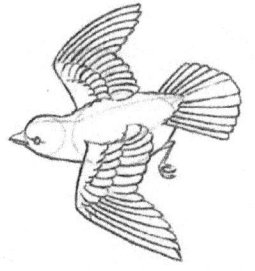

STEP:6

How To Draw a Swallow

STEP:1

STEP:2

STEP:3

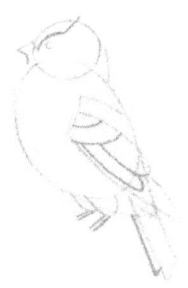

STEP:4

STEP:5

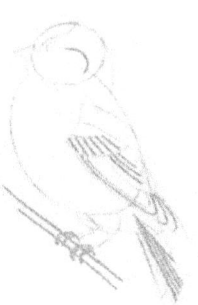

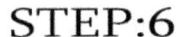

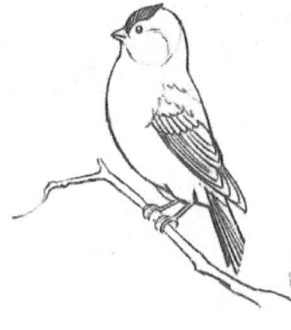

STEP:6

How To Draw Rabbit

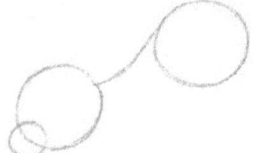

STEP:1

STEP:2

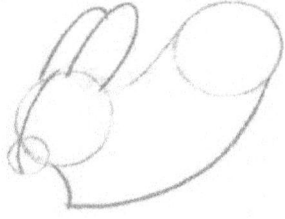

STEP:3

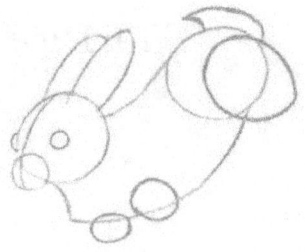

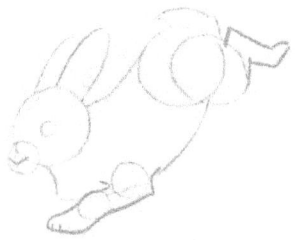

STEP:4

STEP:5

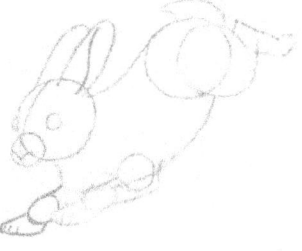

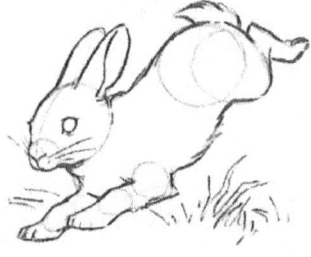

STEP:6

How To Draw Tortoise

STEP: 1

STEP: 2

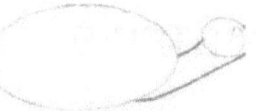

STEP: 3

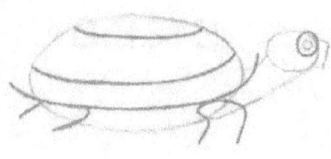

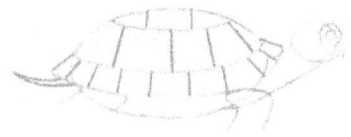

STEP:4

STEP:5

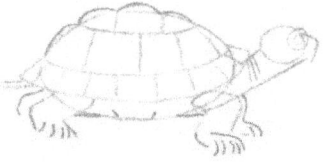

STEP:6

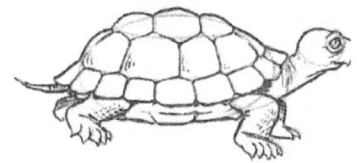

How To Draw Snail

STEP: 1

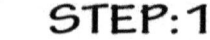

STEP: 2

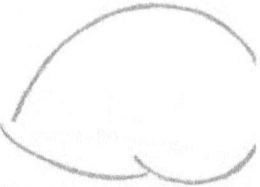

STEP: 3

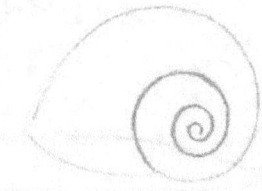

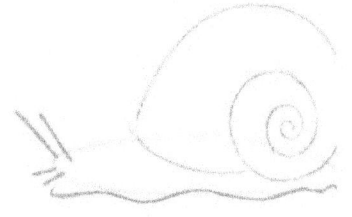

STEP:4

STEP:5

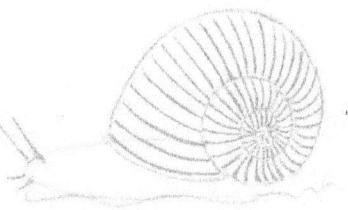

STEP:6

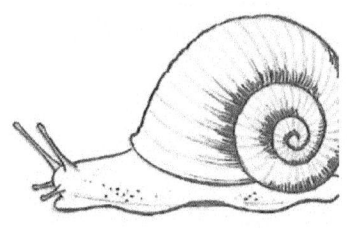

How To Draw Frog

STEP:1

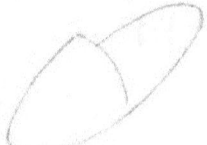

STEP:2

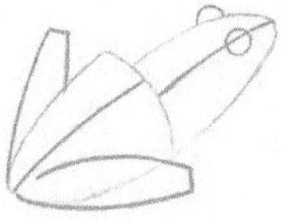

STEP:3

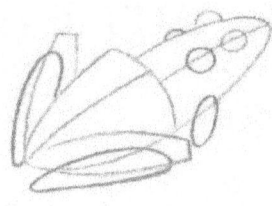

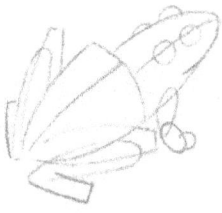

STEP:4

STEP:5

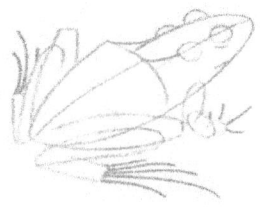

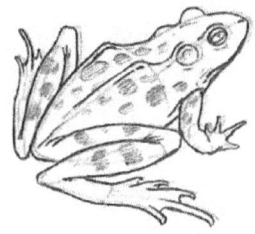

STEP:6

How To Draw Squirrel

STEP: 1

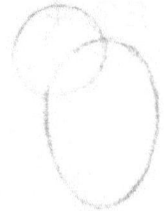

STEP: 2

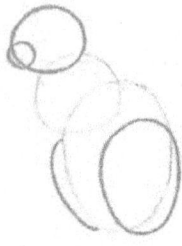

STEP: 3

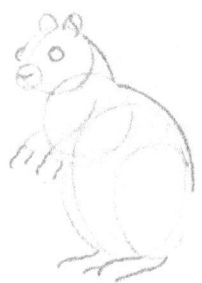

STEP:4

STEP:5

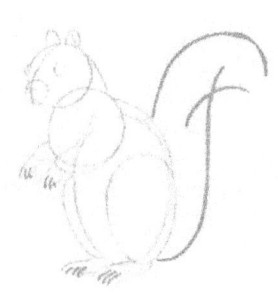

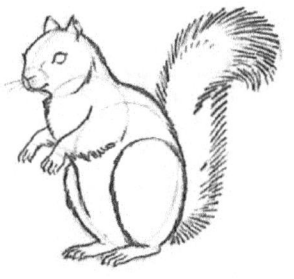

STEP:6

HOW TO DRAW RAT

 STEP:1

STEP:2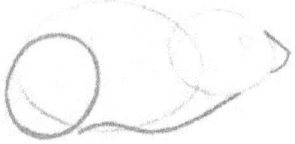

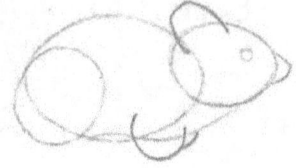 STEP:3

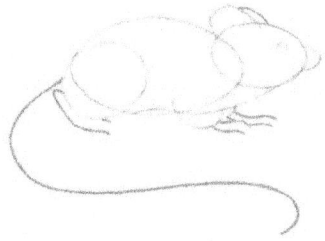

STEP:4

STEP:5

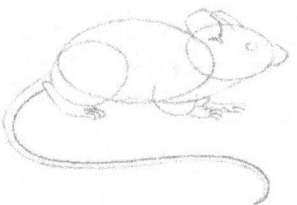

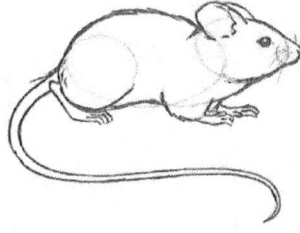

STEP:6

HOW TO DRAW CAT SITTING

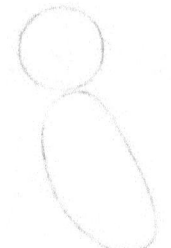

STEP:1

STEP:2

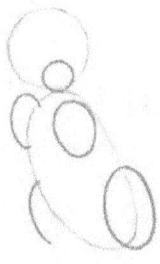

STEP:3

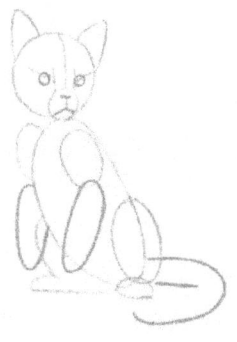

STEP:4

STEP:5

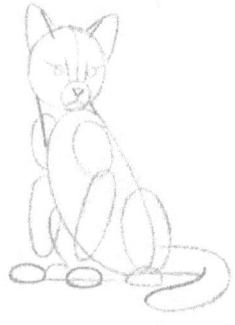

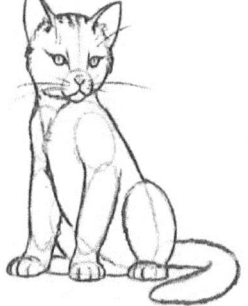

STEP:6

HOW TO DRAW A CAT STANDING

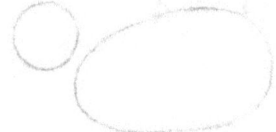 STEP: 1

STEP: 2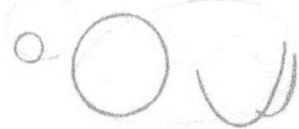

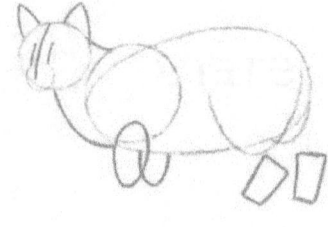 STEP: 3

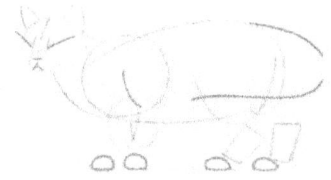

STEP:4

STEP:5

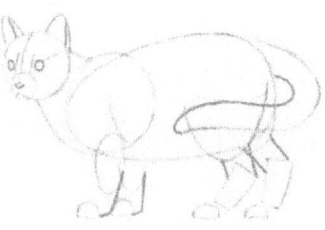

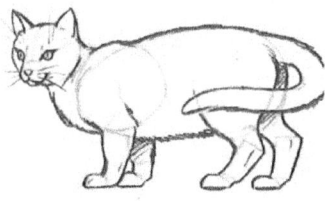

STEP:6

How To Draw Leopard

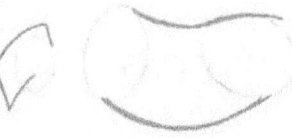

STEP:1

STEP:2

STEP:3

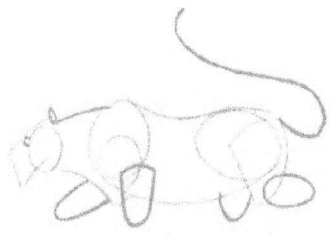

STEP:4

STEP:5

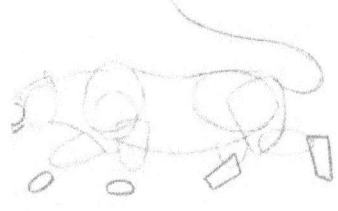

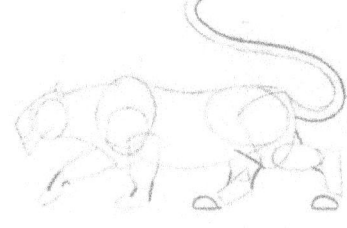

STEP:6

STEP:7

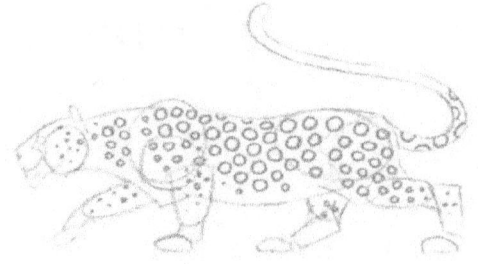

STEP:8

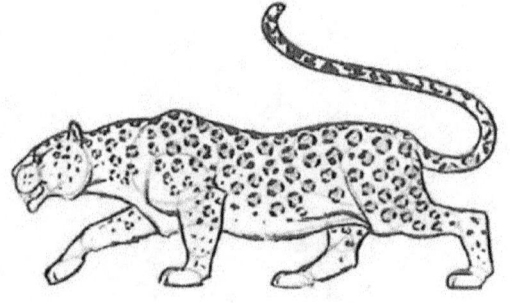

How To Draw Tiger

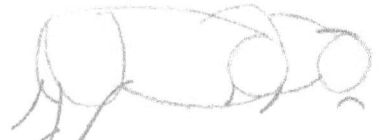 **STEP 1**

STEP:2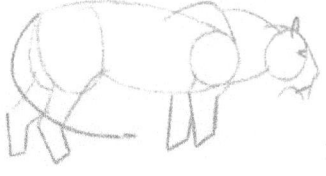

STEP:3

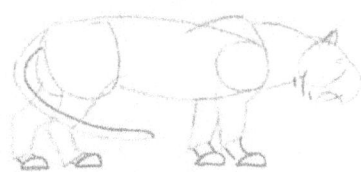

STEP:4

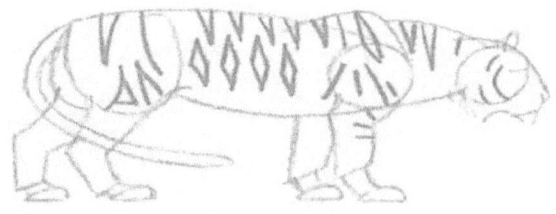

STEP:5

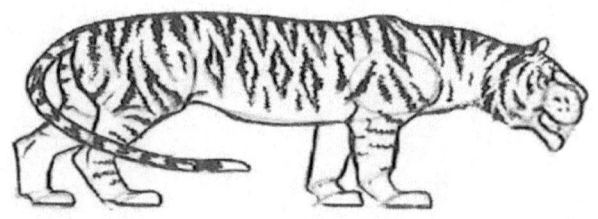

HOW TO DRAW LION

STEP:1

STEP:2

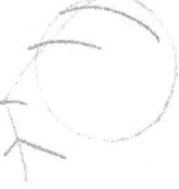

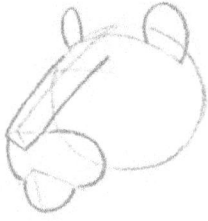

STEP:3

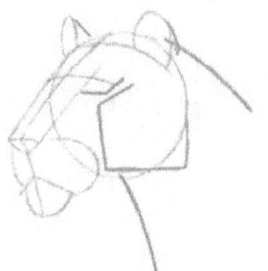

STEP:4

STEP:5

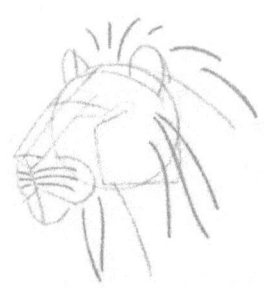

STEP:6

HOW TO DRAW A DOG

STEP: 1

STEP: 2

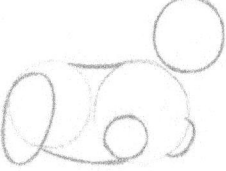

STEP: 3

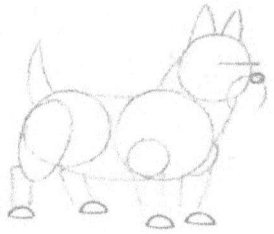

STEP:4

STEP:5

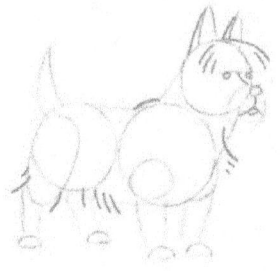

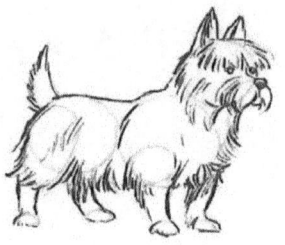

STEP:6

How To Draw Wolf

STEP:1

STEP:2

STEP:3

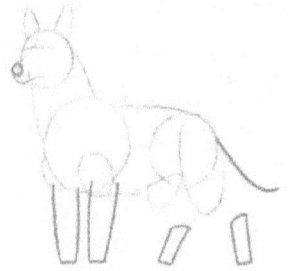

STEP:4

STEP:5

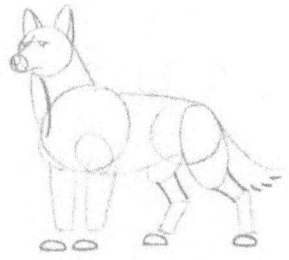

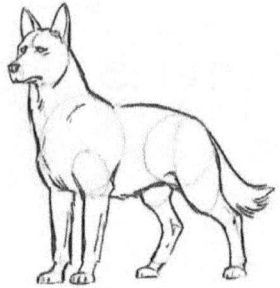

STEP:6

HOW TO DRAW HORSE

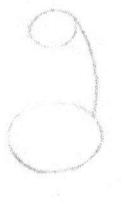

STEP:1

STEP:2

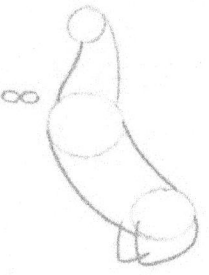

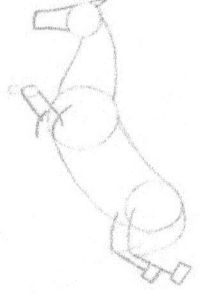

STEP:3

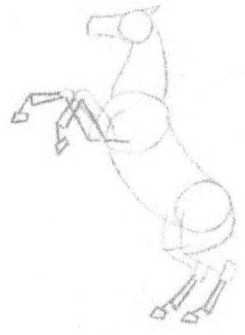

STEP:4

STEP:5

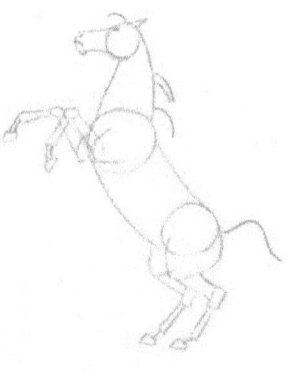

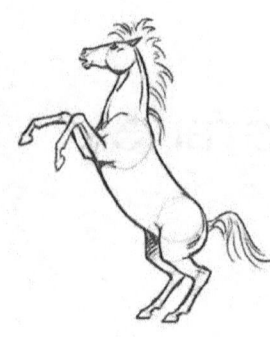

STEP:6

How to Draw Horse Face

STEP:1

STEP:2

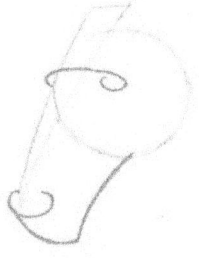

STEP:3

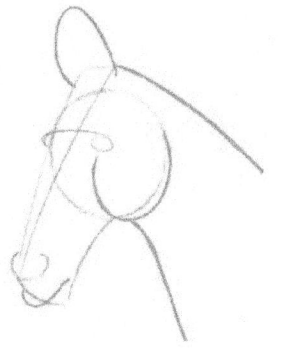

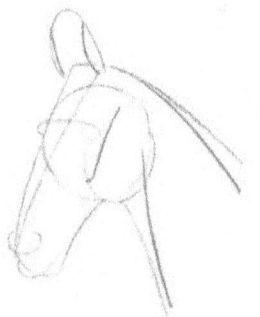

STEP:4

STEP:5

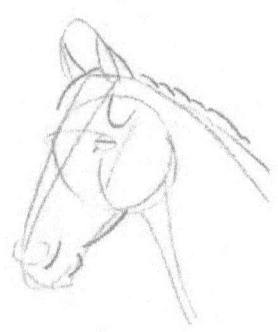

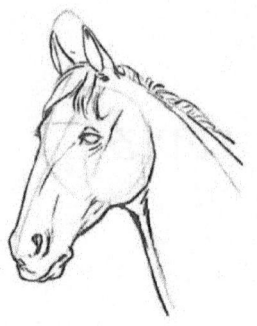

STEP:6

How To Draw Kangaroo

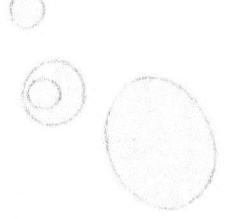

STEP : 1

STEP : 2

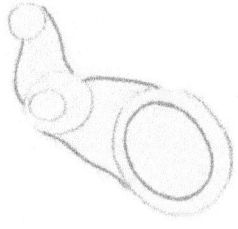

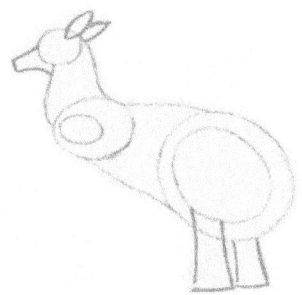

STEP: 3

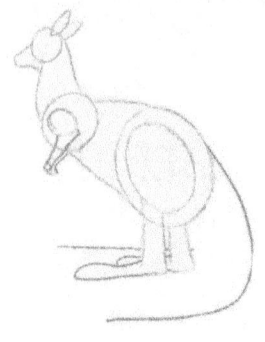

STEP : 4

STEP : 5

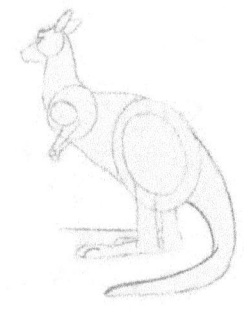

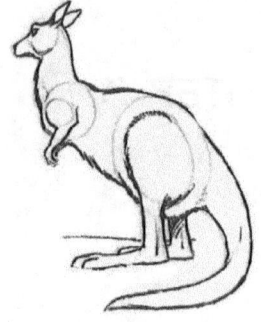

STEP : 6

How To Draw a Beetle

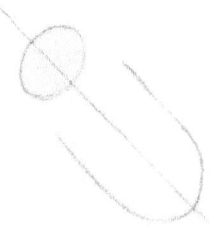

STEP : 1

STEP : 2

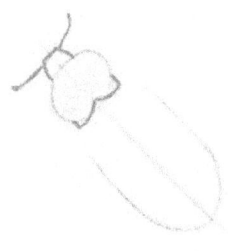

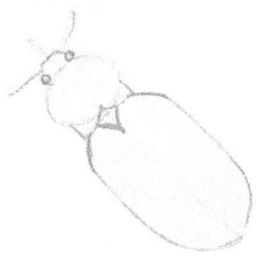

STEP: 3

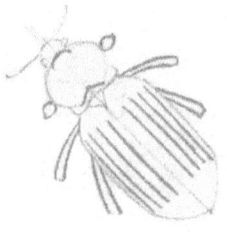

STEP : 4

STEP : 5

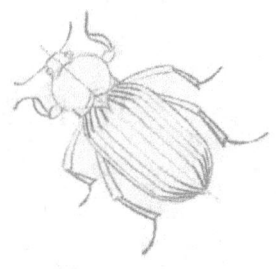

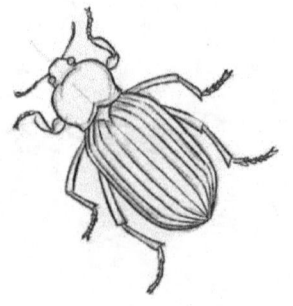

STEP: 6